Discovering
the City

DISCOVERING THE CITY

MERYL DONEY

A LION BOOK

All over the world people live in
cities. They are exciting places.
Some people say it is easy to
forget that this is God's world
in the city.
Not if you look carefully!
Come discovering and you will see.

A city means people: lots of people
living and working together.
Look at the people in the crowd.
Each one is different.

God could have made us all alike.
But he didn't.
Each of us is different and special.

People need places to live and work in; houses, offices, stations, stores, churches...
So cities are full of buildings.
How many different kinds can you discover?

Our cities are full of pictures, colors, and designs.
Everything you look at has been planned and made by someone.

Some things in our cities are ugly.
We can make our cities good places to
live in, or we can ruin them.
A vacant lot can become a garbage
dump—or an adventure playground.

In a big city, people have a long way to go to work and to visit friends. So they have invented all kinds of ways of getting about: cars, buses, trains, bicycles, baby buggies, skateboards... Can you think of any others?

We can even cross the city without
going out!
We can talk to someone on the
telephone, or write letters.
We can send messages by telegram
and telex.
There are newspapers, radio and
television to tell us what is happening.
All these things help to keep the city
alive and working.

People everywhere love to grow things.
We can't grow our own food in the city.
Someone else does that, and we buy it
from the stores.
But we can grow pretty flowers in
window-boxes.
We can plant trees along the street and
make parks and gardens for everyone
to enjoy.

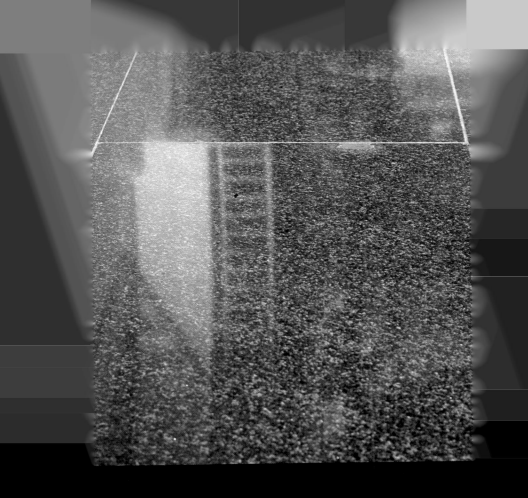

ere are lots of surprises in the city, if
ly we look.
me sidewalks sparkle in the sunlight
e sun is shining on thousands of tiny
eces of granite in the stones.
ese bright colors are made by a
op of oil on the surface of the pudd
e what other surprises you can find.

Cities are such busy places, they soon
get dirty. But when it rains, the city
streets are washed clean. The dirty

water runs down the gutters and into
the sewers, to be taken away to the ocean.
It is God's own cleaning service!

What makes the city such an exciting place? Is it because it's busy, or because there are so many things to do?
A city has special sounds and special smells. Can you think of some of them?

God didn't want us to be alone.
He has given us all families.
Towns and cities are like extra-big
families. But because they are so big
people can get left out.
If we all help one another we can make
our city like a good family.

London   Sydney   Paris

New York   Tokyo   Copenhagen

—every city is different, just as every
one of us is different.
Each one has its good side and its ugly
side.
But the better you get to know them, the
more you will like them.
Just like friends!

Everywhere you look you can discover
the things God has made and the
things he has helped us to make.
When we make our cities good places
to live in we make people happy.
We make God happy, too.
Cities are part of God's world.

Text copyright © 1980 Meryl Doney

This illustrated edition
copyright © 1980 Lion Publishing

US edition 1984
Reprinted 1984
ISBN 0 85648 259 5

Published by
Lion Publishing Corporation
10885 Textile Road,
Belleville,
Michigan 48111,
USA

Printed in Italy

Photographs:

Barnaby's Picture Library: 28 (Paris)

British Transport Films: 15 (railway station)

Robin Bath: 4, 8 (tower block), 10, (fire hydrants), 13, 16 (both), 19, 24 (both), 25 (ice cream van, fountain), 26, 28 (London), 30

Gillie Clutterbuck: 15 (skateboard)

Danish Tourist Board: 29 (Copenhagen)

Elisabeth Photo Library: 15 (traffic), 22

Fritz Frankhauser: 2, 14

Henry Grant: 8 (shop window), 17

Lion Publishing: David Alexander 9, 15 (trams), 28 (Sydney), 29 (New York, Tokyo); Jon Willcocks 3,8, 10 (signs), 18 (window box), 20, 25 (night lights), 27.

Picturepoint: 25 (band)

Popperfoto: 10 (house)

John Sterling: 7

George Thompson: 12

Jocelyn Van den Bossche: 18 (supermarket)

Derek Walker Associates: 6, 8, 11

Robin Weedon: 21